Praise for *Esc*

"In this follow-up to his excellent debut collection, Joshua Robbins simultaneously expands the scope of his imagination and focuses his exacting attention on the deepest questions we face as moral actors in a broken world. Robbins has the courage to get angry with God; to confront Him, doubt Him, plead with Him; to lift our suffering toward His absent face. And he has the greater courage to let God respond in a voice that is by turns frustratingly distant, intimately critical, and violently beautiful, a voice embodied in the 'grackle's throaty ca-chings,' in a mural of the crucifixion on a cinder block wall, in 'the way the setting sun sifts / its burdens down / through the horizon's // Dusty exhalations / and onto the blocks / of vacant houses compliant in their rows / silent and searching / for heaven or stars.' This challenging and immensely quotable collection deserves courageous readers and rewards them with pleasures that go deep enough to hurt."

   —**George David Clark**, author of *Newly Not Eternal*
and Editor-in-chief of *32 Poems*

"With a forgiving spirit, unrelenting, patient eye, and deft lyricism, the poems in Joshua Robbins's *Eschatology in Crayon Wax* render our damaged yet redeemable landscape, and the big sky of their author's heart. Claiming innocence as its baseline, these poems probe our individual destinies as well as our species' and our planet's with ingenious skill. The poems' varied tonalities allow for hope, anger, and resignation to interrogate each other in cascading layers of drama and revelation. This is beautiful, hard earned poetry, a finely crafted gift that I will long treasure."

   —**Khaled Mattawa**, author of *Fugitive Atlas*

Also by Joshua Robbins

Praise Nothing

ESCHATOLOGY
IN
CRAYON WAX

JOSHUA
ROBBINS

Library of Congress Cataloging-in-Publication Data

Names: Robbins, Joshua, 1979- author.
Title: Eschatology in crayon wax : poems / Joshua Robbins.
Description: First edition. | Huntsville : TRP: The University Press of
  SHSU, [2024]
Identifiers: LCCN 2023032960 (print) | LCCN 2023032961 (ebook) | ISBN
  9781680033076 (paperback) | ISBN 9781680033083 (ebook)
Subjects: LCSH: Life--Religious aspects--Poetry. | Theodicy--Poetry. |
  Intermediate state--Poetry. | Piety--Poetry. | LCGFT: Elegies (Poetry) |
  Religious poetry.
Classification: LCC PS3618.O315235 E73 2024 (print) | LCC PS3618O315235
  (ebook) | DDC 811/.6--dc23/eng/20230725
LC record available at https://lccn.loc.gov/2023032960
LC ebook record available at https://lccn.loc.gov/2023032961

FIRST EDITION

Front cover art: "Halloween" © 2023 Bo Bartlett / Artists Rights Society
(ARS), New York

Cover design by Bradley Alan Ivey and Joshua Robbins
Interior design by Bradley Alan Ivey
Author photo by Harper Robbins

Printed and bound in the United States of America

TRP: The University Press of SHSU
Huntsville, Texas 77341
texasreviewpress.org

Eschatology
in
Crayon Wax

Poems

Joshua Robbins

TRP: The University Press of SHSU
Huntsville, Texas 77341

For Arthur Smith, in memoriam

Contents

"Where are his notes I loved?"
John Berryman

/

"Look: hope is a lie."
God – *The Book of Job*

Introduction
by Jeffrey Schultz

Historically, the forms of lyric poetry emerge from the secularization of prayer and sacred language. Prior to this emergence, deep in what the West calls "prehistory," all language called upon the communal spell of sacred image for its powers, all language cast the Spirit's spell. Instrumental language, with its quantitative, discursive, and narrative logics, a form of language which we presently like to pretend is some sort of genetically encoded eternal ideal, or what others would rather call "natural" human proclivities, was unknown, as were the hierarchical priestly-warrior societies that developed these techniques of ideological indoctrination in order to secure and maintain their power. The secularization of language, which historically precedes the earliest inklings of the Hebrew bible by millennia, accomplishes the hobbling of prayer and the simultaneous inauguration of the tradition of lyric poetry. The power of the lyric image, that is, was never so great as it was prior to the emergence of the lyric image proper: the prehistoric realm is the realm of image, and the triumph of history was to place a taboo upon those images, to render them silent and incomprehensible and to declare their enticements temptations of the devil.

The forms of instrumental language that characterize the historical period, forms developed primarily for settling accounts in hierarchical priestly-warrior societies fueled by slave labor, monoculture, the exploitation of animals, and the accumulation of private property, developed its own form of poetic expression, seemingly more suited to satisfy its needs, namely that of the heroic epic. The heroic epic, precursor of today's narrative forms, is itself an extension of the taboo on the gnostic images of prehistory. In this sense, though it is linked to priestly-warrior social structures and modern religious forms, forms which are inevitably implicated in hierarchical domination and social control, epic is, fundamentally, a movement toward the secularization, the despiritualization of knowledge and experience toward the end of constructing and maintaining oppressive class-based societies. We are so deeply immersed in this history that it has become difficult to recognize that the great bulk of what we today refer to as "image" is merely description; we have almost entirely lost the ability to distinguish between the two.

The liberation, then, of lyric poetry from religiosity, evidence of which appears as early as the 7th century BCE in the Greek tradition, is among poetry's most momentous and most dubious accomplishments. Momentous because lyric's liberation from the orthodoxy of the ideological functions of the temple priests opened the possibility of its development as a form of criticism, a quality best glimpsed in its early development in Alcaeus's monodic songs. Dubious because this same liberation severed the lyric image's relation to the communal spirit and tied it inextricably to the individualistic spirit, the trajectory of which has come to inform all of history's developments, through modernity and postmodernity, and which, at this moment, leads us ever-closer to the event horizon of ecological and societal collapse and climatic catastrophe, among other apocalypses.

It is worth noting that this denial of the communal spirit is as true of the choral lyricists as it is of the monodists, however much the performance scheme of choral lyrics would like to obscure this fact. The great tragedy of lyric's historical development as lyric is that it has remained incapable of rising above individualistic univocality. When Pindar arranged his choruses, he did so in the same spirit that the "heroic" warlord landowner might oversee the work of his slaves. The turns of lyric are the turns of individual consciousness and the form of lyric is an affirmation of the primacy of individual consciousness.

With the West's passage from Heroic Olympian to Christian religiosity, the poverty of lyric forms divested of communal spirit, a poverty which, in the context of pre-Christian Rome mostly strikes one as a form of barbaric idiocy (Catullus's rape threats directed against his rivals provide just one example), rises to the level of a true crisis of representation: how, in the context of the Judeo-Christian taboo on images, can the lyric image take any form whatsoever? How can the taboo not be violated in the process of bringing the lyric back to spirit? That little, if any, lyric poetry of any particular quality was produced in the West from Late Antiquity up until the Late Middle Ages testifies to the depth of this crisis. The resolution, of course, to this crisis, is to be found in the image of Christ himself: it is through the precise, historical individuality of Jesus that an image of individual consciousness is elevated to the universal. It was not until Petrarch and Dante that anyone made a particularly serious attempt to accomplish this elevation of the lyric, though they made their attempts guided by the long Augustinian-Thomist tradition of thought, a tradition that, it is crucial to recall, is entirely hostile to gnosis and determined to bring Christian thought into conformity with the Aristotelian logic that is the apotheosis of priestly-warrior religion: secular universal law that resides in the hands of men. Dante dehumanizes his Beatrice through idealization, and then, motivated by a deep desire to resurrect an image of Heroic Olympian individuality, imagines that his ideal would love nothing more than to guide him, personally, toward inhuman ideality, revealing in the process precisely the sort of monster he is. Dante, the great medieval lyricist, succumbs in the end to the failure of the epic form, the ideal poetic form of the ruling class.

The Christian tradition's whole great struggle with the problem of evil unfolds against the backdrop of the logical demand that the universal must be meaningful in a specific positive sense, that it must be beautiful, true, and just, yes, but most of all, that it must be entirely consistent with the established rational laws of oppressive class society. In this light, the Christian lyric form's insufficiency to truth is revealed: the Christian image of the specific historical individual as the universal forms an image neither universal nor individual, but rather stereotyped, mute, though rarely without a lot to say: it is a mirror facing a mirror with nothing in between. Such abstract universality is unable to conceive of concrete communality, which is inherently local, specific, and personal.

This essential problem plagues all great Christian poetry as well as an enormous amount of poetry that would like to think it has nothing at all to do with Christianity but which, because of the enormity of the power of the ideologies embedded in material-cultural history, cannot be escaped so easily as we might hope, and almost certainly cannot be escaped by accident or ignorance when the problem itself has become universalized as an aspect of the form of all popular culture commodities.

It is in the context of this failure of tradition, which has been responded to in any number of ways since the modernists but never really overcome, that Joshua Robbins's *Eschatology in Crayon Wax* appears, and it is in this context that it might be read. Robbins, who in his first book, *Praise Nothing*, used the turns of the choral lyric to reach in the direction of self-negation here turns against the form of the lyric in order to reach toward negation itself.

In *Eschatology,* each poem is paired with an italicized response in a second voice; the first poem constitutes a sort of prayer, an individual consciousness reaching out toward the possibility of the universal, even if only as-if, and the second poem offers a reply from the universal, a response in the voice of God. Robbins adapts this pattern from the psalm-response form of the early Church, and his first voice will be familiar to readers of *Praise Nothing*: it is that of the self-critical and sensitive individual struggling to find expression appropriate to experience, struggling to know what might be said and what might be done in the face of a reality so fallen it is apparently well past any possible redemption.

Robbins's second voice, the voice of God, follows from Berryman's attempts to overcome the univocality of lyric, but, where Berryman stands accused of the same sin as Pindar, Robbins accomplishes the form of his second voice not as an extension of the self into the other as a form of dominating universalization, but rather by constructing a universal voice that so completely negates the first voice, the voice of the modern individual, that nothing but the mute encounter with the incommensurability of what is actually right in front of us remains: what the reader is made to encounter is the fact that something has gone so terribly wrong that nothing can escape wrongness itself, that nothing lies without it, not the self and its attempts to understand, and not even God, a figure who must not just *live with*, these poems tells us, but must also *live through* all of life's injustice and barbarism, all of creation's irreconcilable contradictions, all of its blunt, stupid atrocities and horrors.

It is not that the voice of God is even immune or utterly aloof to Robbins's first voice, a voice often broken-hearted with the intimacies and disappointments and tendernesses of the domestic sphere. God experiences all of those tendernesses as well, but because the world is bereft of Spirit, this God is bereft of Spirit and thus has no capacity to make anything of anything. God is what abides in the most perpetual and painful contradictions: every tenderness is overlaid with overwhelming horror. Historically, the ability to reason away the reality of this horror has been called "being reasonable," and people have been made to accept this despiritualized idea of reasonability as a condition of participating in socio-economic life. Robbins's image of God seeks to reveal and negate this domination, to collapse any apparent logic of existence right back into existence itself, so that logic cannot dominate a recognition of conditions as they are, namely, wrong.

This voice of God is characterized by discontinuities, lapses, a childish authoritarianism, and a sort of hillbilly patois that's conversant in cable news tropes as much as theological intricacies; these qualities render it a knot of contradictions and possibilities pointing in any number of directions, none of which appear to go anywhere. It is a voice that cannot be read singly, but cannot really be resolved into multiplicity of singularities either. While different emphases in reading might highlight different possibilities, what must be remembered is that none of them develop into realization; we are left with an unreconciled mixture of impulses and attitudes and poses. In this, it offers a way to imagine the irreconcilability of the ideal of cohesive, independent individuality with universality. Through this image of irreconcilability inherent in the form of the second voice, the apparent cohesion of the first voice, which is, after all, nothing but the voice of individuality reaching towards its realization in the universal, is obliterated.

The reader who reads these poems sensitively is rewarded with the experience of being placed between the two facing mirrors, and will not cease to be struck by the fact that they have, after everything, no image, no reflection at all.

Eschatology
in
Crayon Wax

Prayer with Rotohammer and Stained Glass

Let my worship
    be this work
and the force
    of each bit–strike

on masonry.
    Forswear my doubtful
tongue. Let
    my past

words be
    what they are:
failed elegies
    to the living word.

Let praise
    be pain rejoicing.
What rose
    like dust

now falls
    and it is beautiful
and meaningless
    and out of time.

Say you won't
    let me go.
In the darkness,
    I close my eyes.

Nothing vanishes:
    clumsy life,
crowded street,
    the perfect I thought

could not take
    me back
for want of it.
    Truth: all remaining

choices are
    as enormous
as what feels
    hardly enough

to make me
    whole. When light

breaks through
    darkened stained

glass, no pane
    can know itself
without the other
    panes. What

I've bargained
    away I can't
explain in words.
    When a stone

is hammered,
    the form of what's
broken becomes
    another form.

yers   *through a glass darkly*   *ain't*
prayer   *I gave you*   *damn near*

everything   *speech*   *slit throats*   *ash*
millennia   *its endless*   *teeth*   *conflagrations*   *I ain't*

lying   *ain't gonna be me*   *lying*
face down   *at the end*   *there's still*

so far to go   *for no good reason*
you'll know it when you see it   *I would*

point it out   *don't turn away*   *like me*
you still don't know why   *I made you*

Eschatology in Crayon Wax

> "It's morning again in America"
> – *Reagan campaign commercial*

October and the Llano Estacado's
               echoless sea of dry grass

mingles with the state's highway dust,
               fall's rumors

of Ebola, and the firmament's half-asphyxiated
               petitions for rain.

In Plainview, I stop for gas,
               drop my last twenty

for a paper and fifteen on pump #3.

The attendant offers his requisite "God bless" and nod
               before I go out to fill.

Behind him the greasy rotisserie turns
               —100% Texas Beef! —
its hum vaguely tempting

and just as clichéd, predictable,

as the radio evangelist's Sunday call-in show
I've been following since Amarillo:

Putin's rise, the Tribulation, RFID,
               and freedom's number of days.

This far south,
               the prophecy's signal is as much white noise
as it is likely,

though the headline below the fold

might beg to differ:
MAN SEES "MARK OF THE BEAST," CUTS OFF AND MICROWAVES HAND.

I remember Children's Church,

coloring in the angel and his bowl of wrath,

the Beast with seven heads,
                                    its seven crowns,

the pale horse and rider I filled with green:

an eschatology in crayon wax

shaded by Gorbachev,
                              the dollar's decline,
duck-and-cover.

And yet, those Sundays, too, were just

another morning in America,
                                    rising then as it did

three days ago
over the aluminum belly

of that off-the-grid Airstream,
                                    its warped linoleum,

and the body
bled out and prepped to rise,

the highlighted scripture open beside him,

something about saints
                              and the trumpet's first fiery blare,

the Morning Star gleaming in the still sky
                                    like Diablo Steel,

its glint beneath the kitchenette's fluorescents
just before the Sawzall's teeth met wrist flesh,

before the makeshift tourniquet

and the bloody thumbprint on the microwave punched to max.

Due east, the caprock and aggraded caliche
rise and fall

                    like an entire history of belief

buried beneath the panhandle's
                              alluvial fans:

everything I'd learned of Eden
and the angel's fiery sword,
                              Nineveh

and the windows of heaven
                              opened,

a Roman execution,

and how all of it
                    was reason enough to fear

a port-wine birthmark, the Rapture, and ATMs.

The pump clicks off and I head in.

Hours from home,
                    I spend what's left on a hotdog, a Coke,
and pocket the loose change.
                              Even now,

my prayer's the same:

trust in the Lord and lean not on my own

understanding
                    of liberty, perestroika, the radical fall.

y'all don't believe in much   so much
has fallen   where's it at   all my names

hold out their hands   longing is
something I can name   & something

I can't remember   to finish   there is no other
life   friend   boring as everything   you've never

asked me   what is beyond finished knowing
then   I once heard   did you now

no argument then   ears to the ground
footsteps   is someone here to carry me home

Anniversary

Sunday's late-afternoon heat
strolls the neighborhood's new blacktop
and dogs the strays
                    collapsed in playground shade

and whatever mercy found the wren
                              and buckled its orphaned heart
beneath the picnic table where I sit taking in
what little breeze comas the live oaks,
                              draws out
laughter from back porches surrounding the park.

Soon, evening will arrive with its darkening refrain
of malt liquor and stars,
                          wafts of agave blooms and marijuana,
all the particulars that give me reason
                              to sing,
even though this year was yet another

call without response
                    from the other world,
what I pray is beyond this dust,
a descant of clear light and purpose
                              where the body
crescendos into the unknowable.

What keeps me yearning?
What keeps you here
                    in this world
of torn light and my excuses?

I want to tell you I'm afraid things do not go on this way,
waking too early, driving to work,
                              and, later,
chopping onions, some wine, soft music to dance to

as the hardwood creaks
and our toddler sleeps in the next room,
                                    dreaming
a familiar melody neither of us will ever hear.

I want to tell you I'm afraid of grave walls,
how I didn't run yesterday,
                              that I'm afraid
I don't love you enough.

I know about the small bills stashed in your favorite books,
that you will wake one morning when the sun's minor salvations seem
just enough and more
                              than what I can give you.

What if I've been here all along,
singing to the same God
                              that is not the same God,
asking for water, for wings to rise,
                              singing *Please*?
I thought by now I'd have something more to say.

Above the rooftops,
                              norteño tunes rise and drift on through July.
What I want is to hear you call me home.
Listen. I'm afraid there is
                              no other world.
I'm afraid this will never be enough.

hand in hand & solitary   yer way
my sword   uninterested   then   a flickering   a trace

blue glow   signal-fade   drifting
into callsign   color bars & tone

later   yer marriage   mostly lost beneath
laugh track   lesser intimacies yer used to

but no longer request   this   one life   namings
grammars to invent   massaging her neck   mon petit chou

love too is a test pattern   & the beauty
yer lives are only passing through

Declining the Angel

On the turn lane median between CVS and Jack in the Box,
    he watches for the traffic signal's turn. In his box:

green crosses and hand-woven rosettes, palm-
    sized angels twisted into shape from plucked palm

fronds. A few commuters waive small bills held
    out the driver's side. Most just wait on green. *I held*

the man for nothing in my arms, I think, and drop ashtray change
    into his hand. I decline the angel. "Keep the change,"

I mutter—mindless quip—which is why the meek shall "Eat the Rich."
    From the backseat, I hear, "Daddy, we did that because we're rich,"

and before I can launch my pious litany about why the new
    insurance won't pay Mom's labs, the bills stacking up, how the new

light-up shoes he's so damn proud of were gifted secondhand,
    we pull forward. "Bye, sir," he smiles, waving his two empty hands.

ain't words enough to explain
my silence   some trope   like water   something

unbreakable   or a myth   perhaps   a cage
a voice in a jar   a lightning flash or mirrored

smoke   see the stranger's eye   regret
even   what it leaves behind   that rush

on certain afternoons   light textured
on brick   buildings long vacant   then

sudden hardhats   machinery   scaffolding
reaching up   plans   you assume

Elegy on New Year's Day

for Arthur Smith

Turns out the new year was no more than a glare of frost
on two squat sabal palms and how they go on

dying a little more each day behind the bus shelter
where someone shaves over a Styrofoam bowl filled with bottled water

even as his breath fills the streets
with fog and the pertussis expands within him

as if it all means nothing because it does not.

And if you listen closely
just after the cross-town's pneumatic doors wheeze shut,

you might hear from his pallid lips a Latin curse
or a few bars of Puccini,

a flame-shaped exegesis on the number of days.

But you have been dead just over a year now and so I hardly think of you.

The palms, having accepted the unacknowledged vicissitudes of God,
will go on dying and dissolving into afternoon.

time is just a shifting of weight from one foot to the other.

  ::

A short walk from where I write this,
Christ in flowering thorns, arms outstretched and attended by two angels,

exhales into morning from his cross painted on a cinderblock wall.

Where even are you?
You must know it's happened. And how ordinary.

In your last moments you would not let go of breath.
Of such things. Of others.

And Jesus raises his arms.

And for what. And who will be raised again.
And these were never questions.

Merely a short list: what you *would* give up and what you *would* keep
for one more anything.
The conditional, in the words of Christ, *is apostasy*. Believing
you could always add something else. One more.

A breath.

   ::

On your last day, you nursed whiskey alone and raked leaves from the drive

and never thought God owed you extra.

Even for the death of your young wife whom he took, breast then breast.

There are some who refuse to stay with the dead.
There are some who cannot choose.

   ::

If the angels in the mural, or otherwise, could choose otherwise,
would they?

Would you?

To rise from a hand-painted hieroglyphic of God's suffering
and to become afternoon's deepening swell above the city?

And what then?

Sometimes I ask, Where *were* you, instead of, *are.*
As if I could go through it all, again. As if you could.

Forget you.

::

The temptation, as I write this, is to go back, put you there in that shelter,
to that first moment of unconscious breath and before the last,

to imagine you there with the sky in no hurry
and the palms and frost

and how it might, finally, go on forever this way,
with you here.

Christ, just one more breath, I would say.
I would say.

either way   you know you can ask
anything of me   I'll give you all's I got

it's trapped inside   thought it'd disappear by now
you too   ever dream a feeling

being lost   almost no part of me
is missing   the whole   from up here   I think

you want all things possible to want   this
is what I'd like   to tear you

however slowly   apart from what I've said
shhhhhh   this you ain't supposed to hear

Apologia Sharpied on Cardboard

What is it that dusk's cobalt last light invokes,
    grimed as it is by grackles' throaty *ca-chings*,

their scrapings and clicks
    protesting this city

and its eradication designs:
    dusted chemicals, poisoned suet,
                    percussion bombs?

And since the horizon's edge of what I owe
                is otherwise
    beyond what I can see
         and, beyond that,

its tenor equally unknown
        and as shapeless
    as pesticides settling on the courthouse steps,

the gridlocked intersection's competing hamburger joints' signs,
    telephone lines and streetlights,
            the bank's whatever trees,

I enter my guilty plea
    and look away from the grit
        ginned-up or steeled

in the face of this man cruising the turn lane's
        stuck sedans
    and hawking yesterday's paper,

the same man whose cardboard sign this morning read simply
    ANY THING HELPS

and I, cashless, offered nothing,
    drove on.

A minute's walk from here,
    the new downtown ordinance prohibits sleeping in parks.

Benches were removed,

the concrete spiked.
The open hand is fined.
No interceding.

What would I see
if I could remove the rearview's
stark reflection
of my excuses?
All of us are hungry

for change,
for angels or fire,
to come clean

to the trinity of words
Sharpied onto cardboard,

all of us begging
for something hidden in the drifting clouds,
to leave everything

behind. After all,
wouldn't your wife make do? Your children?
Wait.

Don't answer that question.
You were talking about poverty, right?
What's prima facie?

And see how easily you returned to necessity
as if it were a thing
that won't outlast the sky?

I am a fool.
Even the birds know it,
rising against business hours,
my necktie

loosening,
my paycheck
auto-deposited.

If it mattered,
    I swear I would apologize

for even thinking the instruments of power
                        deploy a language
    at all separate from anything I might say.
                    And yet,

in a matter of minutes
    I'll be home: the leather sofa,
                maybe a drink,

record my family's daily
          expenses.
    My apologies,
        but men die every

day, the news lacks so much,
    and I no longer believe a poem
            can change anything.

I tell you   ain't just sparrows   but sparrows'
shadows accounted for   same's for glaciers

calving   coral die-off   colony collapse
same's for favored nations   their righteous hands

pulling them levers   alright try this then
drone precision   cluster bomb   wedding

rubble   damage control   all things
I say are possible   I am multitudes

suburban mall   the loaded magazine   each
copper jacket's flash   sparkles from the wheel

For Heaven or Stars

A glory of hyacinth-scented
                                    bronze light
        and a solitary angel intoning the Tao
                                            at the base of a cedar bole,
            latticed wisteria nodding duskward

above the flagstone path inscribed
                                    with prophets' sutras
        flashing like shattered half pints:
                                    your afterlife.
            You knew how it'd be.

And nothing like the unfinished
                                    cul-de-sacs' empty
        spec houses' austerity
                                    stark in early evening's
            onset half-light, the model subdivision's

LED streetlamps long switched-off,
                                    and where you
        swallowed pills, vodka,
                                    before drifting toward whatever
            ruled-out earthly ever after

you'd sought here,
                        but could not find.
        Days before, we stood on the edge
                                    of the dying
            mall garage's rooftop

drinking stolen minis,
                        winged
        our empties at exiting
                                    bargain stragglers, bored
            security on break.

You dizzily skirted the railing's
                        drop,
        your liquor-burned brain already
                                    fevering mania's
            synaptic chemistry, your blue-flamed tongue:

I see God! I am God!
                              Soon after: 24-hour watch,
               restraint straps,
                              forced meds.
               Not enough.

If there is only one world,
                              why is it this one?
               But then, I am
                              not the one
               to whom the Angel spoke

and, besides, maybe Paradise
                              doesn't care
               how you get there.
                              Only that you try.
               And so, I imagine you

behind the wheel, buckled in
                              and letting go,
               the way the setting sun sifts
                              its burdens down
               through the horizon's

dusty exhalations
                              and onto the blocks
               of vacant houses compliant in their rows
                              silent and searching
               for heaven or stars.

here   take this   shape ashes
into ashes   & smear it a bit   there   now

you see   yer a bit dead too
pay it no mind   c'mere   closer   you

done gone & took too much
again   & I ain't wrong   & that ain't not

for nothing   & would you not believe   tender
as I am   & willing   I am   ready

take yer eyes   in the dark   there remains
I promise   a darker   & enough to touch

Still the Dark Field

There was a drone of dying
small engines, a child's toy shovel scraping the drive.

It was late in those early months.
We still wanted everything.

The carport dry rot remained unaddressed.

Remember the folding chairs beneath our bright sneakers,
the ropes' hasty nooses, how dusk
became a cinched wet rag, our mouths cleaved?

There was still glass in your scalp. Still the dark field.
Someone there told me burning bodies hear thunder.

For good measure, let's take our pills. There is ash floating.

Each day we are closer. Don't close your eyes.

this gonna bring you little more than more
the world's a pyre   here   you watch

see the young women set aflame
they are young women set aflame

ℚ why must we go over this   ℚ over
anyway   I'll take what I can get

look   yer questions ain't mine
to answer   cinders rise   disappear   ain't nothing

strange about it   besides   I can't tell
you what on earth I'm doing

Letters Red Like Animal Blood

We posted a large sign:
                    Keep Out!,
        its letters red like animal blood.
And though we put many nails

        into it,
                    you pulled it down.
Nothing we did
        could keep you
                    from us.

We burned
            candles in every corner
        of the house
thinking you feared fire.

        We shouted, "We are sick with fever!"
But you sent a cold wind through our bodies.
        Our teeth
                    fell from our skulls like seed.

In our fatigue
        nothing grows.
                        Months have passed.
Now we argue

        about when
                    you will finish us off.
Even in our dreams
        we wonder.
                    Some nights,

we can hear the bed
        muttering plans for escape.
Closet doors
                    no longer open.

        If we cut off our ears
and offered them
        or scraped out our tongues

and made a paste
                    to smear
        across our foreheads,
would you then
                    pass by our door?

        Though we have heard it has happened
this way
            for centuries,
        we are not comforted.

There is nothing
        you cannot take
away from us.

lemme see here   it appears   you
need only   bridge railing   & drop

sobriety   prayer   dream   songs   all
they're worth   this is the day

that the I has made   & yer soul
sheds yer claustral meat   so to speak

wink wink   slicked   culled   exchanged
figure this   whether lives live

again   I reckon   we do   yers &/or mine
mine   fine   mine   hello   hulloo

Theodicy After City of God

If righteousness remains,
it is moonlight
         glinting
the mica-flecked steps

and waxed lips
         of barren
concrete planters
as midnight skaters' kickflips grind

oblivion
near the courthouse
         sign's
annunciation

where stragglers
         huddle
in a delinquent arc
against the wind's
         cold
dispensation

of *Guilty* and *Not*
in which any
         joke
like *How do you*
         make God laugh?
means

it's time to split
         wheat from chaff,
to let
whoever's
         without sin
pull

from the ashtray's dark
         one more
damp refry
since those who believe
         surely
never die.

when light comes down   that's it   history
don't look at me   them's the rules

ℚ besides   who can't recall
ex nihilo   amiright   no rush   I'll wait   how're you

anyways   last I remember   you began
to think   about me   one prayer

in just a little while   everything gathers   questions
is a heaven   I ain't seen since the start

as I recall   there is an end   ℚ when
it comes   you will no longer wonder why

If Paradise Has Cul-de-sacs

If Paradise has cul-de-sacs,
                              gold-leafed curbs and a gild
on sewer drains and manhole caps,
                              on every structure built

upon a common state of grace,
                              they are not mirrored here.
And so, one tries to make *here* close:
                              this glint on empty beers

from holy dew in curbside bins,
                              and, though it isn't proof,
less golden- than a urine-tint,
                              beyond the tract house roofs,

day's acute light coalesces
                              and one can faintly see
the neighborhood's holinesses
                              without contingency.

So, why should one believe in much
                              of anything? Thomas,
after reaching out, his hand touched
                              God. Any faith came last.

scratch that   good heaven's
foil-wrapped ⊘ stinks   providence

suckles dumpster bags' swollen teats
what meaning here has the wood

the spear tip   the wound   for you   bare
snarl   for you   all's trespasses

the way back is the way forward
the asphalt's heat-haze   overpass shade

no matter   still the only living word
for hunger is hunger   for hunger is hunger

In the Dark Heaven of an Hour

What if we can do no better
                          than this: on our own
    and the only witnesses to the gravel
and weeds we are meant to become,
                      but, for now,

    ignore,
            listening instead
for the world to play the infinite
    song of its last breath
                as space

gathers like the crowd
    at the edge
                of police strobes
and caution tape

    where the mini-mart sign's buzz-glow
casts the assemblers' shifting shadows
    onto hot asphalt

and moon-washed oil slicks
    uniform in their stillness
after the first good rain in months has receded

    just as soon as it fell,
                just as the body
of the late-shift cashier inside the store
    fell out of dream

hearing the entrance bell's
                double-chime
    like the declamatory end rhyme
of an unfinished poem

    penned in his notebook's margins
before dozing off,
    as if he knew the night

could not do
    without us

reflected hours later
in the doors' glass we stared through

    as though through
                our own sleep
broken by gunshots
    at the end of our street
lined with oblivious crepe myrtles
                devoted, in a way
    I cannot understand,
            to this world,
which no pale god watches

    tumble through the universe
as he rocks on his heels somewhere
              in the dark
    heaven of an hour

before bed and too late
    to do anything
            to stop
the thief in the night who pulls

    his trigger twice and puts
one in the gut and one
    in the chest
         of the man

on the other side of the counter,
    who might have told us how
           we are more
than fragmented ruins or shards
          of the ordinary

    things one gives one's life to
and which were already gone for him
    that moment he looked up and out
         and past

this world that kills
    as calmly and deliberately
as a perfect final couplet might
        if we could read it

    now or after we've all
had a drink or a smoke on the porch

to calm the nerves, we'd say,

before morning yields

to the traffic's groans,
        as we shield our eyes
and drive off
                toward nowhere.

I won't just make do with nothing
knowing you & where you are   might you

care now to give up   this dirt
what you buried in the night   all

you got   I'll bury   whatever   this shows
beyond a doubt   I listen to no one

what went on down here is you
shut yer mouth   shut up   all

you got to know is I have heard
what you were saying   it's not for nothing

Confession Through Chain Link and Honeysuckle

Through chain link, twisted honeysuckle nods
        as the Bradford pear's low frequency hums.

    White blooms drip. Bees rim the crammed trashcans' lids.
                I remember the drive's hard concrete, scrums

and pulsing egos, the shut garage door
        Dopplering back the bounce of every called

    bank or swish. Bricks left you open to *fag,*
             jerk, needle dick, pussy, though the strict scald

of denotation was, at best, downright
        lost on me, who'd only ever Frenched flowered

    lips in fogged reflections after late-night
            secret showers had discharged the power

of my blossoming rage. I knew I'd sinned.
        My fear: the hard-bright thing that buzzed within.

c'mere I said ꝙ confess each one
nothing more   best be damn sure

not the razor   not the benzos   stashed
the single-vehicle collision   yes   bless

indeed   the yellow bottle's peach pills
bless yer as neededs   yes   ꝙ bless

not divorced   bless repair   bless thou
shalts   ꝙ thou shalt receive now

this flesh   taken as flesh   open
yer mouth   tongue out   I wanna see you beg

Philomela in Texas

Festooned in tangled
                      plumes of castoff
         silks and costume jewels
                                pilfered from the pile

of my wife's closet's
                      fall cleaning,
         my son dervishes
                         the hardwood

in a frayed tunic
                      destined
         for the second hand,
                            then slides sock feet

to the window
                      of the front room
         where all morning
                            I've been trying to read

about the nightingale's
                      hush, the timid King
         of Athens, Philomela's
                         tongue writhing

in the dirt.
                      It's Saturday,
         Homecoming,
                         and he's watching

begrudged neighborhood
                      high schoolers
         sleepily practice–run
                            the afternoon's parade.

Down our street,
                      a flotilla of diesel–growling
         pickups cruises
                         hot asphalt,

crêpe paper streamers
                  rippling
      off side mirrors
                       and tow hitches,

piloted by boys
                  slunk low
      as their regally chiffoned
                       counterparts

balance
                  shaky heels
      on the beds'
                  jerking steel.

"But I'm
                  the Queen of Texas!"
      he declares to me,
                  five years old,

his left hip
                  thrust out
      and right hand raised,
                  monarchical.

Over his shoulder,
                  a mockingbird
      scissors the too-soon
                  humidity, harvests ants

from the dead
                  St. Augustine runners
      near the base
                  of the barren pecan,

then hops down
                  to bathe
      in storm drain
                  backwash,

wings outspread,
                  as if to shed
      a self not itself.
                  I remember

his face
              that one morning,
       his first word, *Bird*,
                     as a fist-sized

juvenile preened
              in the gutter-dust.
       What I grasp
                     of fatherhood

is always less
              than what I thought.
       He is innocent
                     and radiant

in his mother's clothes.
                     If I could,
       I'd eat him piece
                     by piece.

here's the secret   I'ma whisper   destroy
one of everything   that mockingbird   window glass

curiosity   that name
you swallowed   feel how it grows

at the edge of the neighborhood   its blade
serrated   either way   it's gonna work

out for me   hush hush
do not misunderstand   thou shalt

choke on the bones   don't you
forget it now   make it believable

After Miscarriage

Ten o'clock and the just-closed big box sign's
    electric glow still bathes

the lot's white parking stripes a sickly pink,
    not unlike the inexplicable buttonweed

blooming out of the accumulated mix of shoppers' detritus
    and autumn's sporadic runoff,

its sediment collected outside
    the culvert's forever-hollow maw

above which this strip mall sleeps, dreaming,
    if it does, of balance transfers

and point-of-sale withdrawals.
    Every choice has a cost.

And maybe if I'd listened, rushed you to Emergency,
    something there, someone,

To stop your bleeding.
    And maybe if I stand here long enough

for an accumulation of dust to gather on the windshields
    of every parked minivan and family wagon,

maybe I'd have enough to shape
    some bleak meaning

out of your loss, restore to your mouth
    the name you repeated

through clenched teeth
    as I drove you too little

too late and the possibility of saving it
    became a darkness

over the city streets and blind
    to my useless hand in yours.

the sign's broke   strip mall neon throbs
Mira—Mira—Mira—Mira—Mira—

look   no miracle   myrrh & gall   asphyxia
spear-tipped stars in disregard   blood-water

not even the dust anticipated that ending
amiright   & who now could wait

weeping & apart   for that stone to roll
pray for nothing   what you seek

is already yours   what you
seek is already yours   what

The Fire Thief

Dogwood winter stunts
    even the wavering roadside
bluebonnets and switchgrasses,

    the radio newsman warns
of black ice, and seven
    thousand miles from our

Texas valley snooze,
    Prometheus, imprisoned in Caucasus
snowpack, clatters his chains.

    It seems our waiting
will never end.
    Your mother does the time:

doctors and lab work,
    revising our list of names.
As if to coax

    the tiny flame of you
into our world, we spend
    our afternoons

making love. My fingers
    trace the third trimester
globed circumference of you.

    What emerges from love
begins and ends and begins
    again in the inexplicable.

How like the wheeling
    raptor's shadow–steel
scalpelling, even here,

    the curved gleaming belly
of the earth beneath us.

can't dispute it   turns out you need me
yeah yeah drop to yer knees   like the rest

there is another world   & you've waited
so   somebody'll come you said & here

I am   as countless as what stars blah blah
blah blah blah   on this side

of the dark   sometimes the effect's both its own
cause & end   you can speak   hush

what's this about really   the light
it seems   it's finished   is there another way

Held Up

Taped-up hearts red as IV gauze-blooms
               burst behind the new

      credit union's streetside plate glass reflections

of hoppers hauling coal and twisted scrap
               south toward Laredo's railyards

      and I'm first at the gate's gravelly edge,

high strung, prepping grief,
               held up hustling back

      to the Methodist NICU

where my newborn son screams
               or sleeps, bound down

      by tangled tubes, his mother's ever steady

and exhausted hands.
               Nothing to do now

      but wait, count cars, inventory the night

bag I rushed to pack for her,
               cotton panties, hoodie,

      her mother-of-pearl earrings from the bedside,

the new toothbrush I forgot
               after the second shot I knocked back

      and left to water stain

the day's mail: past dues
               and pre-approved credit offers,
      grocery coupons, a direct mail

sweepstakes scratcher: EVERYONE'S A WINNER!
               Think of anything else, I tell myself:

the tight blue scrubs of the overnight nurse,

scuffed light pooled on the linoleum
                    outside the ward's newly empty

room, that childhood cartoon villain

twirling his paternalistic black mustache
                    as the engine steams closer.

Last night, I watched a family on our floor

pass around a newborn's unhooked
                    and swaddled body. No cry.

Inside the room, muffled wails

as the abuelas in the hall
                    swayed, whispered songs

in Spanish, placed the child

into the father's stoic arms.
                    He crouched there, deliberate,

set his sweat-stained straw hat

on the floor,
                    then stood, then raised

the still fragment of all he'd lost

up toward the momentarily silent
                    speakers. In the near distance,

a train blared.

His boots' chrome tips flashed
                    and did not move. I walked back

to our room, my hard chair.

you could not remember   yer tallness or thinness   you would
                          not have seen you   had there been

a mirror   you could not remember   yer bedroom   or where
                    the ceiling was supposed to be   yer wife

                gone   glasses   papers & desk   clock
            vase   thumbtacks pinning postcards to walls

                walls gone   the window   doorframe   door
you could not remember   the sound of yer voice   if you did

or did not have shoes   the grocery store   where you worked
            yer nightly walk   which road to anywhere else

Ash in an Empty Room

Every day there's more
                        and less of your name
in this room and always plenty
                            to do. I speak your name

and dust the sills, the toys,
                        smooth cold sheets,
refold the soft shirts
                    into which I'd stitched your name.

How can it be
                    that you've left this world
when all of you remains?
                            Even the ash has your name.

I read the labeled box,
                            surround it with your playthings
on the shelf, family portraits
                        that won't change. Rename

me. Ask me once
                    again, again and again,
to play that game, to open
                        my hand and guess the name

of what you make me hold.
                        No. *Made* me hold.
A truck. Your doll. You'd laugh.
                        Never the right name.

What is today? How long
                    must I wait? Tell me.
when can I close the door
                    on the empty room of your name?

g'on & grieve   beloved   all the years
you believed   so   so much

for change   & who cannot recall   longing
it's damn foolish   but why not

to have been created at all
this ain't no gentle dream   as I know

you know   make me keep my word   grinding
away   a way   little one

you're trying to understand   the naming
well   trying's got nothing to do with it

Rope Swing

When my son said,
             Daddy, this rope

is a door,
             and the pecan's

sickled leaves silvered
                         green

above the highest branch,
                         the one I reached

only the day before,
                    teetering atop

the topmost rung
                 of a borrowed ladder

to tie a knot
             as baffling to me

as a Texas breeze
                  on certain mornings,

like those
          when a three-year-old's

metaphor
        hangs in the air

suspended
          by nothing,

I knew
      I must move through

the narrow space
                leveraged there

by his tiny body.
                 There was no way

to know
         when the beauty

he opened
         would close.

              ::

And in the same
         moment,

I remembered
         my friend

in high school,
         who had no rope

and so
         wrenched together

wire hangers stolen
         from his father's closet.

He had enough
         to fashion

a loose noose
         around his neck,

hang it
         from a park bathroom stall

doorframe.
         I swore

I would never tell.
         His attempt failed and now

the failure
         of my promise

hangs from the end of the y
         at the end

of his name.

And swings like a rope

across this page,
                    its sound

that unanswerable
                    question and the door

we all must enter
                    if you believe

there are answers.
                    If you believe

there are
          questions.

                    ::

When asked why
                he paints only

the anonymous bodies
                        and not the rope

that hanged them,
                    the artist

at the downtown gallery opening
                                said the absence

of a noose
          is the threat

of a noose.
          And so, each man floats

against a blank canvas,
                        caught in an erased

instant,
        as if struggling

to keep
        in focus

as each contortion's
                    unwritten history

opens a truth
                    of which I know

nothing
                    and cannot enter.

The impossible facts
                    of their bodies.

                    ::

And so how can I refuse
                    to write this:

before he tried himself,
                    he took me

to the same park
                    to see

where they'd found
                    a man hanged

from a red oak.
                    And, man, he said,

around his neck,
                    was like this rope

of blood.
                    Soon after, we watched

the fog's white hands
                    descend

over the police,
                    the dispersing crowds.

Where we went after,
                    I don't remember.

                    ::

If beauty is truth
                    and so on,

and if it exists at all,
                    it will not

be found
          in these whispers

of graphite
               pressed and moved

slowly
          across this blank page,

because no matter
                    its curve or closed loop,

a letter
          is not *like* a rope, it is *not*

a noose.
          Even the idea of it—

blood rope—written down
                              is nothing

compared
          to the sound

of fibers stretched taut
                         by a man's weight.

the body   its memory   weigh nothing   & are
nothing   & only die   once   & on

the other hand   only die   once
I told you   don't expect too much   otherwise

I could do worse   whatever you thought
you were called   to do   to be broken

in all directions   I did nothing to help
you   I gave up   God   the real

possibility   ain't no heaven   for mine remains
the judgement & the slaughter & the glory forever   amen

Vanity, Sayeth the River

Plastic marigolds propped
    against the new hospital wing's chain-link

lift their throats and orangey silks
                        in the downtown wind.
    Faint tang of bus diesel.
              Mash whiskey.

A graffitied Emergency Room dumpster rises
    into another sleepless weekday dawn,
                  October's ashy smolder.

I watch the municipal truck's pneumatics' metallic shudder.
    There is no emptiness beyond empty.

Restless in the visitors smoking area, I lie
    back on the table's polished concrete

to clear my head of arrangements,
    who gets first call.

Maybe Death's pale fingerprint
    is a TBI clot eight floors up,
              my father's induced coma.

I imagine whoever left
            the ersatz memorial,
    their slow waking,

then the sound of rough broom strokes
    over the kitchen's longleaf,

chorizo frying in a black pan,
    as a thin breeze nags

the front room ofrenda's draped linens.
    Sepia-toned daguerreotypes
               stare out

of the familial dark
    toward a plug-in candles' faux-flicker glow,

a pour of dollar-store wine in its squat jar,
>   stale pan de muerto
>   >   on chipped bone china.

nonetheless,
>   the apogees of memory set up
>   >   and ignite their altar

behind my eyes:
>   a sleepless night's
>   >   migraine flash

and my father calling to say
>   he knows
>   >   how he's going to do it,

how one pull of the wheel could end it—
>   moonlight-flare, concrete median,
>   >   cliffside drop—

how the payout's large, so long as insurance
>   is kept in the dark.

In the ICU,
>   there was talk of surgery,
>   >   global aphasia,

the "waiting game"
>   and the "wait-and-see,"

all the clichéd tonics
>   that linger like cedar pollen

coating the table,
>   the bench at my feet,
>   >   the hoods of parked cars

sleepily turning over
>   to join the unwashed masses'
>   >   early stop-and-go.

When I first looked down at him,
>   the fluorescence, for a moment,
>   >   seemed

to kiss him,
        his stillness,
                    the way

Death's dusty lips might press
                        their final seal
        onto an exposed wrist or bald ankle,
                            his just-shaven cheek.

Vanity, sayeth the river,
                    blocks away,
        All is vanity,

its trash-fire gleam
        rolling without concern

past the gravel park-and-ride lots.
        In the near-distance,

the long-haulers
                    rattle their chains
        and the graveyard drunks weave home,

the east-west upper interchange's two-lane
                            transcendence
        just getting started.

when the wine's blossom-sweet purples
yer tongue   when the wafer   when lilac

nods against stained glass   when I
become a might bit less necessary   when

yer soul's lifted by early shade
live oaks cast across the dying

lawn   when a single grackle   silent
feasts on what you cannot see   yer faith

how grave   beauty's in the wings
iridescence   its beak   a scythe

Exchange

It begins always with what's soon gone:
                                        a fleeting apparition,
            some neurochemical
                                firing deep
                within the gray matter's
                pathology of need.

It is why the body of the speculator
                                        falling now
            from forged steel
                                        and into the open palm
                of the churning river below
                knows all there is to know

of value
                and why the billboard on the bridge railing above him
            whispers
                                        the one pragmatic sweet nothing
                    we all long to hear:
            AVAILABLE.

                                ::

And it is why any allegory of desperation
                                        must first
            be wrenched
                                        from the calloused fists
                of Those That Don't
            before it can be transferred,

with deference,
                        into the soft
            expectant hands
                                        of Those That Do.
                Brokenness and regret
            are worth as much shattered plate glass

or a brick's weight
                                landing on the lacquered
            floor inside the mini-mart
                                        as they are

the hunger of the woman
who threw it.

And all remains
                    meaningless
until demand sets in.

                    ::

                              But for now,
        the man falling
is still a man

and is yet as meaningless
                              as the sky,
        which seems somehow suddenly
                    permanent
        like the way two long constellated
indigo stars tattooed

on the skyless,
                    freckled,
        inner-left thigh
                              of a woman
        I'd fallen for, how they return in memory
as if out of that blue. How it is

as if pressing my lips to them now
                              wouldn't cost me
        everything. As if

                    ::

                              it would. As if every
        moment,
even one as insignificant

as this,
        someone standing awash
        in gas station fluorescence and diesel stench,
                              has its asking price,

that the gears of common disaster
are oiled

by the prayers of those who've lost.
                                    The world is falling.
            ::

    The world is falling and this afternoon
                    one errant key stroke
            concealed by cubicle walls
        sent wholesale systems of mutual exchange

into digital collapse.
                    A single fat finger
        depresses *B* as in *billion*

                not *M*
            as in *million*
        and on Wall Street

Di Modica's *Charging Bull*,
                        stuck good, bleeding out,
            torques its horns to gore
                    and hurtles headlong
            toward the pecuniary abyss.
        As confession, cries of *Buy* or *Sell*

are meager substitutions for remorse.

                        ::

                            But no matter.
    Even now, the Big Board scrolls and glows
                    ever bluer. As blue as the sky
            over the river now
        or over gray

Manhattan sidewalk in 1929,
                        Black Tuesday,
            when the ruined
                        leapt from ledges and prayed
            in their descent that, for a moment,
        the sky would be willing

to exchange
            what they knew they'd done
        for whatever oblivion

it could offer.

But if confession
is worth nothing,

::

what did it earn her then
when she told me
she was beaten as a girl by her father,
how anything was a motive—poor
grades, forgotten laundry—
how once she accidentally let fall

from her hand the electric iron
and so, as if out
of the blue,
he held her down and pressed
its hot aluminum soleplate
against her leg.

Because he *had to*. Because
I love you.
For that, what wouldn't be a fair wage?
Why not incise proud flesh
with ink where metal burned,
make permanent all that losing makes?

::

Don't deny it. Every
thing
transacts. Always has:
barley for corn and rock salt for sea-,
the first ox-hide-pressed
copper ingot for trial-and-error's

blistered palms,
and, now, the Express Pay's binary code,
its digitized *chirp*,
for the debit account's swiped plastic
as the pump's electric numerals blink
and the woman behind the register

counts down her till. Another day sold
for seven dollars
an hour at the far-flung periphery
of single-zoned sprawl,

where even desire's most casual
manifestations triggers in each of us

a nerveless shiver of want.

::

Inside the mini-mart,
condensation's invisible hand ghosts the cooler glass
as the high-gloss unconscious of capital
drifts
on an odor of citrus-scented industrial cleanser,

which lands like a kiss upon the lips
of the bored waiting
to fork over their cash.
Above the checkout, the nightly news is stocks,
a local suicide,
and beamed-in highlights of uproar overseas.

Again
the ritual exchange:
skull crack for the blackjack's stun,
the riot shield for a jawbone dislodged.
In hi-def,
does the coin-like aftertaste

Which the brain
synthesizes
in the instant before consciousness
fades and the body drops
reveal itself as blood
or as something more real?

If there were a stench
of paraffin burning
as the helmeted phalanx closed,
would we know it?
Above the megaphone's command,
chopper blades *thwomp* the contours

of moonlit cobblestone and teargas plumes
and we go on watching
as if value's vanishing point
will never fall
below the horizon, as if
this exchange could go on forever.

Acknowledgements

Some of these poems, sometimes with different titles or in different forms, first appeared in the following publications: *32 Poems*: "After Miscarriage" and "Ash in an Empty Room"; *The Account*: "In the Dark Heaven of an Hour"; *Anti-*: "Exchange"; *Birmingham Poetry Review*: "Held Up" and "Rope Swing"; *Blackbird*: "Eschatology in Crayon Wax"; *The Cortland Review*: "The Fire Thief"; *The Freeman*: "Anniversary"; *Michigan Quarterly Review*: "For Heaven or Stars," "[here take this shape ashes]," "Philomela in Texas," "[here's the secret I'ma whisper destroy]"; *San Antonio Express-News*: "Written in Letters Red Like Animal Blood"; *Image*: "Prayer with Rotohammer and Stained Glass" and "Theodicy After *City of God*"; *New Madrid*: "Apologia Sharpied on Cardboard" and "Confession through Honeysuckle and Chain Link"; *Open Plaza*: "[yers through a glass darkly ain't]" and "[ain't words enough to explain]"; *Spiritus*: "If Paradise Has Cul-de-sacs."

May thanks to the editors of the publications where these poems, and others, have appeared. Thanks to J. Bruce Fuller and everyone at Texas Review Press.

Thanks are due to the University of the Incarnate Word English Department and the Office of Research for grants that provided time during which many of these poems were written.

Special thanks to Jeffrey Schultz, Michael Levan, Jason Willome, Rebecca Hazelton, George David Clark, Lisa Ampleman, Wendy Barker, Natalia Treviño, Alexandra Van De Kamp, Gerard Robledo, Octavio Quintanilla, Christian Anton Gerard, and Laurie Lamon.

I especially thank my fiercest editor, Emily Myers Robbins, for her support and encouragement, as well as my sons, Harper, Caedmon, and Søren, who inspired so many of these poems.

Notes

Epigraph: John Berryman, "Dream Song 28." Stephen Mitchell's translation of *The Book of Job.*

"Eschatology in Crayon Wax": The epigraph is from Ronald Reagan's 1984 political campaign television commercial titled "Prouder, Stronger, Better." The original headline "Idaho man sees 'mark of the beast,' cuts off and microwaves hand" was published by the Associated Press, January 8, 2008.

"[*y'all don't believe in much   so much*]": John Berryman, "Dream Song 14." Emily Dickinson, "340."

"[*hand in hand & solitary   yer way*]": John Milton, *Paradise Lost.*

"Elegy on New Year's Day": The mural is Mike Roman's "Salvación," San Anto Cultural Arts, painted June 20, 1998, San Antonio.

"Apologia Sharpied on Cardboard": William Carlos Williams, "Asphodel, That Greeny Flower."

"[*I tell you   ain't just sparrows   but sparrows'*]": Matthew 10:29-31: "Are not two sparrows sold for a penny? Yet not one of them will fall to the ground outside your Father's care." James Wright, "Saint Judas." Walt Whitman, "Song of Myself, 51" and "Sparkles from the Wheel."

"For Heaven or Stars": This poem is for Damian Westfall.

"[*lemme see here   it appears   you*]": Washington Avenue Bridge in Minneapolis, Minnesota, where John Berryman committed suicide.

"Theodicy after City of God": St. Augustine, *City of God.*

"[*scratch that   good heaven's*]": T.S. Eliot, "The Dry Salvages."

"[*the sign's broke   strip-mall neon throbs*]": Miracle Video, Lawrence, Kansas

"Rope Swing": Vincent Valdez, "The Strangest Fruit," series of paintings, Artpace, San Antonio, 2014.

"Exchange": In the "flash crash" of May 10, 2010, a trader incorrectly placed an order in billions not millions, a "fat finger" error, which caused a sudden and severe drop in U.S. stock indexes. It was later found that the drop was caused by a high-frequency trading algorithm and not human error. Arturo Di Modica's "Charging Bull" (1989). The bronze sculpture near the NYSE is a response to the Black Monday stock market crash in 1987. On May 5, 2010, as many as 500,000 people, by some estimates, marched through Athens protesting the government's austerity measures. Protestors were met with brutality and violent police tactics.